Divine Love

Collection of Love Quotes.

Written by s.hukr

Divine Love

Publisher: Fajr Noor © 2024

All Rights Reserved

ISBN: 9780645766691

Designed & Authored by s.hukr

Website: fajrnoor.com

Divine Love

Salam.

I hope you find peace, wisdom, and love through these words. I hope this book inspires you to love yourself, educate yourself and become a better Muslim.

May Allah guide you toward that which is best while making your Dunya and your Deen easy for you.

If there is a word that you do not understand, simply search the definition of the word on Google.com.

e.g. "Define [word]"

fajrnoor.com

Divine Love

Your beauty is stuck in translation,
when you become a woman in every
sense of the word, my heart felt poems
will be understood.

s.hukr

Divine Love

You think attention is love no
wonder you suffer so deeply.

s.hukr

Divine Love

I hope you learn to love the part of
you that you keep buried away.

That is the part of you I love the most.

s.hukr

Divine Love

How do you expect to arrive at
the most beautiful destinations,

if you aren't willing to let
go of this Dunya?

s.hukr

Divine Love

The fragrance of your Haya lights
up my existence with a breeze of joy.

s.hukr

Divine Love

Give me your stubborn heart or
die in my memories. My love
surpasses the realm of this world
because the place I intend to travel,
I want you there with me for eternity.

s.hukr

Divine Love

I hope you have a beautiful day,
don't work too hard and don't
overthink everything.

Remember to smile, it's the
most beautiful curve of your body.

s.hukr

Divine Love

It's okay to be vulnerable, to be soft,
to admit that it's hard and to have
someone help you.

What kind of ally would I be if I
didn't help you in your time of need.

s.hukr

Divine Love

You are a soft feminine woman who would do anything for a man who takes care of you and loves you with passion.

s.hukr

Divine Love

May Allah turn your frown upside down and ignite your heart with eternal sunshine.

s.hukr

Divine Love

Have sweet dreams and don't let
anyone steal your peace away
from you.

You have a caring heart,
rare amongst our generation.

s.hukr

Divine Love

Him: Don't miss me too much

Her: Who said I will miss you?

Him: The angels on your shoulders

s.hukr

Divine Love

Be kind to your sister.

This is a difficult one especially if she has moods that swing like a pendulum or if she talks so much that you wish she had a mute button.

Be good to her, be generous with her, be gentle and be honest even if that honesty hurts her. I swear she will appreciate it more than a lie that comforts her.

s.hukr

Divine Love

Talking to you made me lose track
of time. I feel better after speaking
with you.

I am alive once more. Your smile
has become my fountain of youth.

s.hukr

Divine Love

You deserve the moon and the stars,
someday you will find them in
the palm of your hands.

s.hukr

Divine Love

I saw you with my heart and not my eyes,
I didn't dream of you, I felt your glow.
I experienced your presence.

I knew it was you.
That is why you were the
most beautiful of creation.

s.hukr

Divine Love

Next time you feel like you're
world is falling apart, message me,
I am only a text away.

s.hukr

Divine Love

If I told the moon what I felt for you,
it would abandon the sun and the
ocean and start following you.

s.hukr

Divine Love

I think a woman's greatest fear is
to be stuck in a union with a man
who is incapable of love.

Love is more than just respect or
understanding, it requires something
deeper and more intimate.

I think most people know
nothing about pure love.

s.hukr

Divine Love

You are a beautiful joy and delight.
My heart flutters into existence
in your presence.

I might be a poet but your beautiful
eyes are the poem that I find myself lost
within. Stay away from me, my words
may bewilder your heart and make
you drown in ocean of love.

s.hukr

Divine Love

Date Idea:

We do our Nikkah, destroy our phones and work together to leave behind a legacy for our children and for our Akhirah.

s.hukr

Divine Love

Make her smile before you kiss her,
so you can taste the joy of her happiness.

s.hukr

Divine Love

If you ever want to marry an Arab girl,
just tell her that she looks like her dad.

If she asks what feature, say her anger issues.

s.hukr

Divine Love

Poetry is the language of how you speak with women whom you adore and admire.

The reason most men don't speak this language is because you're ugly.

s.hukr

Divine Love

How strange to dream of you when
I'm wide awake. How strange to compare
you with the moon and stars.

How strange to write about you so
deeply that the one who reads,
begs to be in your presence.

The moon and stars try their best but
they cannot compete with your beauty.

s.hukr

Divine Love

How beautiful is the heart of those who go through the worst storms in life and still choose to stay gentle, patient and humble.

They win twice – here and hereafter.

s.hukr

Divine Love

Fun Fact:

Gaining people's trust is
easy when you don't lie.

s.hukr

Divine Love

Real beauty is modest and real wealth is silent. **Real wisdom** is heavy and real peace is expensive. **Real love** is a gift and real happiness is worship.

And your presence in my life has been an abundance of joy and delight.

May Allah keep you happy.

s.hukr

Divine Love

"I get lost in your pretty eyes every
day you adorn yourself with modesty"

Is what the husband said to light
up his wife. So, in return she
cooked his favourite food.

And now I have your attention,
make sure to read Quran today.

For if you have Allah,
you have everything.

s.hukr

Divine Love

I love the sound of your smile. I love
the fragrance of your handmade dinners.

I love the modesty of your eyes. I love your
Fajr Noor abayas. I love your luxurious locks
covered in your colourful hijabs.

I love your voice when it recites the Quran.
I love your mindset when it aligns with
the sunnah. I love the weather inside you,
it brings me so much peace.

You are my beaming light in
this my world of darkness.

s.hukr

Divine Love

Sometimes the hardship doesn't come to an end. Sometimes the intensity of pain increases. Sometimes it gets darker and darker. Sometimes it seems there is no way out.

Hardship comes one after another, and you wonder what if it's a punishment?

What if it's not love but a punishment from Allah? But if it's causing you to sing the praise of Allah, to yearn for Him, to cry to Him and to rely on Him and Him alone, then how could this be a punishment?

How? It's love, pure love.
It cannot be anything else.

s.hukr

Divine Love

I hope one day you will smile and say:

"Ya Allah, this is more than I prayed for"

s.hukr

Divine Love

I'm sorry but feminine women have
my heart, those who don't want to have
a career but have children instead.

Those who have Haya and a tender heart.
Those who don't want a big wedding
but want to go to umrah instead. Those
who dress with elegance and whose
beauty comes from Deen.

Please share with me your dark brown
eyes so I can drown in them.

s.hukr

Divine Love

Talk to me about Islam and I will fall
in love with your company.

Tell me about yourself, so I can
discover what makes you so attractive.

Show me your love for your ambitions
and let me admire you from a far.

And in your presence, let me find
beauty in your comforting heart.

s.hukr

Divine Love

I had to block your number because
the urge to text you and make you my
wife wouldn't go away. I want to swim
in your dark brown eyes and drown.

s.hukr

Divine Love

Be a strong woman.

So your daughter will have a role
model and your son will know what
to look for in a woman when he's a man.

s.hukr

Divine Love

Marriage is a status symbol for women they love to put in their bio and on their fingers until their marriage becomes undesirable.

For men the status symbol is having a nice car or talking to many women or having wealth until such things fade away with time.

But I think the best kind of status symbol is to be known in the 7 heavens and be completely hidden in the world.

That requires a divine love.

s.hukr

Divine Love

Taking a woman out of her masculine era
and putting her in her feminine energy
is a real man's job, not for silly boys.

s.hukr

Divine Love

"What's your favourite type of girl?"

I smiled and said:

"The artwork covered in a veiled of Noor"

s.hukr

Divine Love

Stop waiting on men to validate you.

You're pretty. You're smart. You're interesting. You're worth time & effort. You deserve to be loved.

You need to know these things and truly believe in them. Don't wait on some man to come along and tell you what you should already know.

You are a Muslim woman.
That means something.

s.hukr

Divine Love

I crave for things this Dunya could never deliver. So, I have made the hereafter my destination and God my tour guide.

s.hukr

Divine Love

Learn to love. Love for the sake of Allah. Love for God will never blind you, will never betray you, will never hurt you, will never confuse you or lead you astray.

It is made from an abundant Noor that will remain forever pure. It is a guiding light that will always lead towards what your soul deeply desires.

s.hukr

Divine Love

Women respond to praise and
men respond to criticism.

Learn each other's language, it will
save you a lifetime of translation.

s.hukr

Divine Love

The sky is my canvas.
The soul is my ink.

Let us write poetry until our
books are filled with good deeds.

s.hukr

Divine Love

Half of beauty is eating healthy and having some form of physical activity. The other half is the light of your Eman and character.

s.hukr

Divine Love

I pray you find someone whose soul
clings to yours like you have known
them for a thousand years.

Someone who becomes a blessing to
your heart and helps you to attain
the highest level of Jannah.

s.hukr

Divine Love

Fall in love when you're ready
not when you're feeling lonely.

s.hukr

Divine Love

Her weakness is cats, laughter, care,
kindness, gifts, time, love, loyalty,
affection, understanding, attention
and patience.

Give her all that in reasonable terms
and she will give you the world.

s.hukr

Divine Love

There is no such thing as wrong time, right person or right time and wrong person.

It's always the right time and right person.

That is how much Eman you need in Allah. How can we say it's wrong time when Allah is the best of planners? You must acknowledge that every degree, every second of your life is planned by Allah and that you are exactly where you need to be.

There is reason you meet certain people and go through certain things.

You need Tawakkul.
Trust in Allah

s.hukr

Divine Love

It doesn't cost you anything to give your parents sweet words. To give your time to people. To listen to their problems and pray for their success. Be generous in a world that is stingy.

Give and Allah will give you more.

s.hukr

"And whoever is protected from the stringiness of his soul – it is those who will be the successful." 64:16

Divine Love

If you look at the people in your circle
and you don't get inspired, you don't
have a circle. You have a cage.

s.hukr

Divine Love

Women speak a different language,
they will say they aren't hungry but
still expect you to bring something.

The quicker you learn their language
the easier your job becomes.

s.hukr

Divine Love

Half the people I meet bore me to death.

Where are those souls who have
lived a thousand adventures?

s.hukr

Divine Love

The reason I don't show my face is because I don't want girls dreaming about me and in my DMs wasting their time. I'm doing you'll a favour.

Be grateful.

s.hukr

Divine Love

Sometimes you need to flip the script.

Be that man that leaves her on seen
and waits for her to make the move
because deep down you know you're
an irresistible lollipop.

s.hukr

Divine Love

Loyalty is a very expensive gift,
don't expect it from cheap people.

s.hukr

Divine Love

You are too intelligent and kind-hearted
to fall in love with someone who just
wants Dunya and not Deen.

s.hukr

Divine Love

You are more beautiful than the
Turkish language could ever describe,
this is why I have started to learn
Arabic in secret.

s.hukr

Divine Love

Nothing is more attractive than a
woman that admits she wants you.
Her shyness doesn't get in the
way of making things halal.

She replies fast, doesn't leave you
on seen, shows how much she wants
you. She gives you time, loyalty and care.
Who does anything to please you and
only has eyes for you.

She is the most valuable joy of this
earth. She is the type of woman you
want forever.

s.hukr

Divine Love

The presence or absence of a man in
your life does not determine your value or
worth. But it may determine your peace.

s.hukr

Divine Love

You're busy doubting yourself while
so many people are intimidated
by your potential.

s.hukr

Divine Love

"Are you a good man?"

The good man replied: "I don't know".

The bad man replied: "Yes I am".

s.hukr

Divine Love

Marry a poor man with rich character.
His tongue soft even in anger.
His eyes glowing with Haya.

s.hukr

Divine Love

Your doubts and hesitation will inflect your labour of love. Have full Tawakkul in Allah even if you make a great mistake. People admire the confident not the insecure.

People admire sincere ambition.

s.hukr

Divine Love

Arranged marriages is your parents
rizzing up your spouse for you since
you have no game.

Come on brother, be a man.
Come on sister, be a woman.

s.hukr

Divine Love

It is not your responsibility to fix the bad behaviours of others. You are not responsible for the choices other people make. Learn to ignore what is not in your control.

I have never tried to amend the destiny of others for I am no God, I am a simple man.

s.hukr

Divine Love

You are a lucky woman if you have
my attention because ignoring
women is my hobby.

s.hukr

Divine Love

The reason you shouldn't marry a
Pakistani woman is because she
has too much Nakhra.

s.hukr

Divine Love

Your eyes were like Afghanistan,
they couldn't be controlled.

That's why I left you.

s.hukr

Divine Love

A red flag is when she has 3 holes in her nose. Be careful she has breathing problems.

s.hukr

Divine Love

My sorrow heart is filled with untold stories. Yet love will always flow even in the middle of the Sahara Desert. My water has made a Nile in your remembrance.

s.hukr

Divine Love

Make it a habit to understand the people around. The better you understand them the more appropriate the gift you can get them.

Don't buy gifts that people desire, for desires turn into unnecessary problems. Instead get gifts that people need or can benefit from.

That's where the magic happens. Gifts are a form of love. In return you expect only to receive a good deed from Allah.

s.hukr

Divine Love

I think fathers lose their minds a little
bit when they realise that their daughters
are not as forgiving as their wives.

I think mothers love their sons more than
they should because they slowly fell out of
love with their husbands.

I think sons grow up immature because of
a lack of responsibility upon their shoulders.

I think daughters grow up insecure because
of inadequate love from their family.

s.hukr

Divine Love

There will be men who want you
and men who deserve you.

Know the difference.

s.hukr

Divine Love

I find myself yearning for things
this world could never deliver.

My soul does not allow me to rest
and the sorrows of my heart remain.

Until I receive my book in my right hand
and my eyes rejoice upon seeing paradise.

s.hukr

Divine Love

Her: What if you get sick of me?

Him: I won't, you are the artwork
      I could admire forever.

s.hukr

Divine Love

Don't beg people for anything.

If you really want something in life,
ask the one who is always watching you.

And never be hopeless, you will either get
exactly what you want or something better.

s.hukr

Divine Love

Maturing is realising that someone challenging you to be better is not an attack, it's an act of love.

s.hukr

Divine Love

You don't **need** parents,
you don't **need** friends,
you don't **need** siblings,
you don't **need** a soul mate
But you **need** Allah.

When you have Allah,
you have everything
even if you have nothing.

s.hukr

Divine Love

I'm sweeter than honey and more fragrant than musk. I could make your heart flow like rivers of eternal bliss. You will find security, peace, and love flowing through you.

But this same tongue has the capacity to confront your ugly ego, insecure heart and ignorant mind with the absolute truth that you desperately hide from.

I can be your best friend or your worst enemy.
The choice is always in your hands.
And my lord is never unfair.

s.hukr

Divine Love

I can read your sadness from your eyes even when you're smiling.

s.hukr

Divine Love

The wives of the Prophet are the examples that women need to follow.

Khadijah R.A would donate her wealth to the Prophet. She would go out of her way to comfort Him. She didn't marry him for protection or for wealth or for status or luxury, she married him because of His outstanding character.

She was the first to believe in Him. She didn't leave Him when people mocked Him or when he would go through harsh realities. She remained loyal until the end.

She ignored the Dunya in order to serve a man who was committed to Allah. How many of woman would approach a man and marry him because of his Deen and character like Khadijah R.A?

I think many of us are lying to ourselves.

s.hukr

Divine Love

Help people in silence, love people in silence. The world doesn't need to know how good you are.

Allah knows and that's plenty.

s.hukr

Divine Love

I love you and respect you enough
to keep my distance. I don't need to
always be with you. You remain
forever in my thoughts.

s.hukr

Divine Love

Not every man with a heart is understanding, not every man with ears is a listener and not every man with eyes is able to see.

So if you ever find a man with such qualities, while he is on the right path, don't ever push him away.

s.hukr

Divine Love

She is both sweet and sour. The flavour
you taste depends on how you treat her.

s.hukr

Divine Love

Peace is a luxury no amount
of money can ever buy.

s.hukr

Divine Love

The older you get, the calmer you become.
Life humbles you deeply as you grow old.

You realise how much nonsense you wasted time on. You begin to accept things as they are right now. You stop forcing friendships and relationships and just learn to grow.

s.hukr

Divine Love

Love can be fake,
it can be real,
it can be reckless.

Love can be distant,
it can be dangerous,
it can be blind,
and it can be painful.

But I think the best kind
of love has to be pure.

The sort of love that makes
God the centre of your existence.

The type of love that never hurts
but instead grows in perpetuity.

s.hukr

Divine Love

How can you love God
when you don't know Him?

How can you love God when
you don't read His book?

Did you know the first word
revealed is Iqra = Read?

How can you love without sacrifices?

Most of us are not lovers,
but there are lovers in this world.

If you're not one of them, you
must be in awe of them.

s.hukr

Divine Love

If a man cries about a woman, it means
she won't find another man on earth
who loves her like him.

s.hukr

Divine Love

Sometimes all I want to do is spoil
you. Is that too much to ask?

s.hukr

Divine Love

You cannot expect true love when your life is entertaining Shaytan.

s.hukr

Divine Love

Romance is like Rizq, it is not
granted to everyone in this Dunya.

s.hukr

Divine Love

Don't marry a complete stranger.

Marry someone who is known by the angels and by Allah.

s.hukr

Divine Love

The more you fall in love with Islam,
the more you will see your world
revolving around faith.

The closer you will become to Allah.
The harder the tests will become.
The greater the reward for your sacrifices.

s.hukr

Divine Love

Marriage is a responsibility and love is
the sweet reward of your sacrifices.

s.hukr

Divine Love

When you make Dua for someone,
you are offering them the most
purest kind of love.

s.hukr

Divine Love

Shaytan likes to cause separation between people by making us assume bad of others. Don't let him divide us more than we already are.

s.hukr

Divine Love

To be desired means nothing.
To be understood and deeply
loved means everything.

s.hukr

Divine Love

She asked, "What are your intentions with me?" I smiled and said:

"I only want salty coffee from your sweet hands."

And now that I have your attention, go read some Quran today.

s.hukr

Divine Love

The poets were always right.
We just never understood until
it was too late.

s.hukr

Divine Love

Women are funny.

They study 4 years for a degree,
work another few years and then
realise their life is happiest when they
have a man in their life. When they aren't
working a job or chasing the world.

They realise they should of spend the
last 10 years of their life trying to make
themselves wifey material and being
closer to Deen. To educate themselves with
Deen, not Dunya. Women are so funny.

I'm so glad for Surah 4 verse 34.

s.hukr

Divine Love

The reason why Majnun died is
because he loved Layla more
than Allah. Rookie Mistake.

s.hukr

Divine Love

There is a big difference between gifts and favours. A gift is from the heart, it comes with no strings attached.

When a man gives his wife a gift, he should have zero expectation that she should also give him a gift in return.

A favour is something you give someone but have an expectation that they will return the favour one day.

Most people send gifts and expect something in return, this is not gift, it is a Trojan horse. I hate this. I hate how people will trade favours but there is actually no love between people.

s.hukr

Divine Love

You know what's funny?

Women will do all this effort,
wear makeup, do her nails, get her
hair done, shave her little beard,
dress cute, get those flamingo lashes
and even get henna on her hands.

And still feel insecure on the inside.
Absolute clown energy.

Funny because if she put this much
effort on her internal beauty, she would
actually get the validation she needs.

s.hukr

Divine Love

Allah doesn't care about the non-Muslims. He gives them whatever they want because he doesn't want to spend time with them.

But Allah loves the believers, those who stay loyal to Allah and make constant sacrifices and efforts to please Allah. Those that live a very difficult life but stay grateful and thank Allah for every hardship, every uneasy moment. Because they know that to Allah belongs everything and Allah can test us in whatever way he wishes.

Haven't you noticed how people in hardship are always closer to Allah than those who have a very easy life? Just look at the Prophet's life, he was the greatest man to have ever lived yet went through hardships upon hardships.

Was he ever ungrateful? Did he ever complain to people? Did he compare himself to those around him?

s.hukr

Divine Love

People always want a real relationship,
a real man or woman. But when they
get one, they run away from it. Why?

Because a real person will not tolerate your
laziness, your ignorance, your bad behaviours,
your lack of effort and drive to be better.

A real person will hold you accountable, will
make you uncomfortable and will push you
towards bigger and better things.

I think people love the idea of love
and not the reality of love. They love
the dream and not the destination.

s.hukr

Divine Love

How can I love a woman who
doesn't love Allah enough to
wear the Hijab and to pray Salah?

How can a woman love a man
who doesn't pray Salah and who
doesn't seek knowledge?

Both are not worthy of real love.
Love requires sacrifice and trust.
Love requires loyalty and respect.

If you can't love Allah, I cannot
love you in the same way. Pure love
requires, pure hearts and sincere intentions.

s.hukr

Divine Love

Loyal men do exist.

They are busy building their empires,
hidden from reality because that's how
they work best, but what are you doing?

Be the wise woman who can identify such
men and empower them. Pretty women are
everywhere, but how many are wise and young
and absolutely committed to God?

I hope you become one of them.

A woman's success lies in choosing
and empowering the right men.
Please understand this.

s.hukr

Divine Love

I once made a feminist fall in love with me
and then whispered in her ears softly:

"I want 4 wives", even though I don't.

That's how toxic I am.

s.hukr

Divine Love

Let me tell you a secret about women.

They love a calm man practicing religion.
A man with Haya, with principles and values.

They love a man who can be soft but also fierce when he needs to be. They love men with boundaries. Who can provide emotionally, financially, spiritually, and mentally.

It's very difficult for them to say no to man of character, a man of Allah.

s.hukr

Divine Love

Be grateful if you never been to the clubs,
never had a girlfriend, never had alcohol,
never had tattoos, never did foolish
things that most young people do.

That is a blessing from Allah.
Be thankful for it. Because Allah
can misguide you at any moment.

And never think you are better than
those who have a sinful life. For they
could be better than you on
Judgement Day.

s.hukr

Divine Love

The more makeup she wears the more
ugly she is. Beauty doesn't need attention,
it must be covered, as commanded by God.

s.hukr

Divine Love

Do not fall in love with people like me.

I will take you to places you never could visit alone and kiss in every beautiful way.

I will make you taste love in ways you never felt before. I will spoil you in the most beautiful ways possible.

And when I leave you, you will finally understand why storms are made for this Dunya.

I will ruin your love for this world, it will never be the same when you listen to music, when you talk to others, when you read poetry.

For in your heart, you will constantly be reminded of me.

s.hukr

Divine Love

If a man says 50/50 or makes you pay for something, that isn't a man. That's a woman dressed like a man, run the other way sister.

s.hukr

Divine Love

Women are the true driving force behind all men. Find a woman whose sole purpose is loving you. Not because of your wealth, your strength or anything temporary.

A woman who loves you for your faith and the character that it encompasses. A woman who is monumentally impressed by your commitment to Allah. And it is your purpose to make that easy for her.

s.hukr

Divine Love

I never thought I'd see the day
when a girl would send me flowers.

Women are powerful, if only they knew.
They have the ability to select the best
leaders and discard incompetent men
and their lineage.

s.hukr

Divine Love

If this Dunya and all its treasures were
handed to me, it wouldn't do to me
what your eyes have done.

s.hukr

Divine Love

Nobody will love you like your parents.
Even if they don't love you like you
want them too.

s.hukr

Divine Love

Once the heart becomes a beautiful
place, everyone will want a piece of it.

But you can't. You must protect it. You
must not allow anyone to destroy it.

To keep a place beautiful, you
can't share it with everyone.

s.hukr

Divine Love

I found peace knowing that people
are at war with themselves,
not everything is about me.

s.hukr

Divine Love

If I had daughters, I would raise them
with so much confidence and education
that their beauty is heard and not seen.

And I would raise them with love of Deen
such that their aura is strong, they have
no difficulties walking this earth alone.

I want them to be so confident and
secure in themselves that proposing
to a man whom they deemed worthy
is not a difficult thing.

s.hukr

Divine Love

I find most people boring.

They chase money, culture and worldly enjoyments. They lack purpose, passion and love overflowing like a spring.

People like me aren't easily impressed because we are looking for things outside this world.

We have studied about the joys of the hereafter. This world in comparison is nothing.

s.hukr

Divine Love

If you have Sabr with
your family, then it is love.

If you have Sabr with
others, then it is respect.

If you have Sabr with self,
then it will generate confidence
and Sabr with Allah is part of faith.

s.hukr

Divine Love

My heart wants her.
My mind wants success.
My soul wants peace.
Who shall I listen to today?

Without success she doesn't want you.
Without her you won't find peace.
Without peace you can't focus on success.
What is the key to this riddle?

As a man all you need in life is Allah.
For if you have God, you have everything
even if you have nothing. But if don't have
God, I feel very sad for you even if you have
everything in this world.

s.hukr

Divine Love

Love is when:

She covers her body so no one
can see her attraction but him &

he lowers his gaze so he can't
see any women but her.

s.hukr

Divine Love

A real woman knows:

How to be obedient
How to be modest
How to love
How to lower her gaze
How to choose the right man

s.hukr

Divine Love

Islam does not uphold the idea of a
young adult or an adolescent age where
you are transitioning from being a boy to
a man or a girl to a woman.

That itself is a western idea where from
the age of puberty till the mid-twenties,
a person is allowed to make misguided
judgments and act foolish without being
held fully responsible.

It is the western society which promotes
the idea of allowing someone leniency just
because "they are young, and they are bound
to make mistakes and mess up. Teenagers will
be teenagers."

There is no such luxury in Islam.

s.hukr

Divine Love

Fajr is a blessed time when you're starting with success, while others are dreaming of success.

s.hukr

Divine Love

O Women.

Allah dedicated a whole chapter named after you. You are that valuable.

Your rank is high. It is your modesty, your honesty, your kind and loving heart that makes you a queen in Islam. Your beauty is not defined by your appearance, rather, it is defined by your heart.

s.hukr

Divine Love

Beautiful people don't ask for attention.
Beautiful people don't need to wear makeup.
They don't need to expose their
body for attention.

Insecure people do that.

s.hukr

Divine Love

The young boy said:

"I don't believe in love at first sight."

The old man smiled:

"You will when you see her."

I saw Paradise hidden in her eyes and when she spoke, I saw her dance in my heart. She knew the depths of my soul better than I knew myself. She was everything I prayed for and more.

s.hukr

Divine Love

Shesha Smoker: Do you trust me?

Me: How can I trust a heart that is clouded by the whims and desires of worldly life?

s.hukr

Divine Love

Never hurt women. Never yell at them.
Never give them a reason to fear you.

Handle ever matter with love and patience.

s.hukr

Divine Love

Sometimes all I want is to lay in the
lap of my lover while she plays with
my hair and recites her favourite surah.

s.hukr

Divine Love

Research shows every girl has 4 different personalities, 1 for each week of the month and this is why I have developed 16 different personalities.

Some say it's a personality disorder, I say it's my way of keeping her emotionally satisfied.

s.hukr

Divine Love

Maybe if we chased Allah as hard as
we chase people, Allah would grant
us people who we didn't have to chase.

s.hukr

Divine Love

What a shame it is…

We are so quick to find our soul
mate before we take time to find
and truly understand our own soul.

s.hukr

Divine Love

If I ever meet you again, whether in
this world or the next, know that ever
since we parted our ways, my lips have
never tired of praying for you.

s.hukr

Divine Love

Marry a person who prays 5 times.

A person who is guided in matters of Deen and Dunya. Not neglecting either. Beauty fades, wealth runs out, fame disappears and lineage can end.

But Deen is something we will all be questioned about.

s.hukr

Divine Love

Live your life in a way that you do
difficult things only for Allah.

Not for people, not for family, not
for culture, not for your whims and desires.
But for the sole purpose of pleasing Allah.

Do we really love Allah or do
we love something else?

s.hukr

Divine Love

I will choose you for your Deen
rather than your wealth. Your Eman
is what will interest me and not
your physical appearance.

s.hukr

Divine Love

Love isn't logical. Love doesn't
listen to reason. Love doesn't ask
for attention. Love is irrational.

Love is unexpected. Love will fight
the world even if it cannot win. True
love is when God is in the centre
of your heart.

s.hukr

Divine Love

You cannot please everyone.

If you're a friend of everyone,
you are an enemy to yourself.

s.hukr

Divine Love

Princess treatment is good, but life
is no Cinderella story. Don't expect
any man to fall in love with you before
marriage, because if he does then one
of you is the red flag.

s.hukr

Divine Love

Be delusional when you make
Dua because Allah will grant it or
give you something better.

s.hukr

Divine Love

Allah alone gives success.

So don't ignore the call to prayer,
don't ignore the one who can give
you success. Follow His religion
like death may visit you tomorrow.

s.hukr

Divine Love

O Allah, move me from the humiliation of disobeying You to the honour of obeying you.

s.hukr

Divine Love

Children get excited over new toys.
Teens get excited over new experiences.
Adults get excited over new relationships,
but souls reminisce of a life after death.

s.hukr

Divine Love

This generation is very fortunate to have the latest cameras to photograph the wasted years of their lives in the highest quality.

s.hukr

Divine Love

Don't let the first day you wear hijab
be your last day on this earth.

s.hukr

Divine Love

Do you love the idea or
do you love the person?

If you love the idea then you will
be disappointed over and over again
but if you know the person and adapt
accordingly, you will love the person.

s.hukr

Divine Love

Not every Muslim woman has a hijab
but every pious woman has one.

s.hukr

Divine Love

Long hair turned into short hair.
Dreams turned into responsibility.
Laughing turned into silence.
A boy turned into a mature man.

s.hukr

Divine Love

Thank you for reading this book.

I hope that you enjoyed it and
found some benefit from my words.

May Allah always have mercy on you
and guide you towards the straight
path. **Ameen.**

Sincerely,
s.hukr

*P.S If you love this book, please promote them, and
share it with others and maybe you'll earn a good deed.*

*P.S.S If you liked this book, you should checkout
my other books.*

fajrnoor.com

Divine Love

S.hukr Books

1. Fajr and Noor

2. Through His Eyes

3. Noor upon Noor

4. Slice of Paradise

5. Mumin Mindset

6. How to Marry a Muslim Girl

7. Divine Love

www.ingramcontent.com/pod-product-compliance
Lightning Source LLC
Chambersburg PA
CBHW031251290426
44109CB00012B/525